The Holy Sacrifice
of the Mass

Barbara Reed Mason

*All booklets are published
thanks to the generosity of the supporters
of the Catholic Truth Society*

The Bible quotations in this booklet are from the *CTS New Catholic Bible* published in 2012 by The Incorporated Catholic Truth Society, unless otherwise indicated.

All rights reserved. First published 2023 by The Incorporated Catholic Truth Society, 42-46 Harleyford Road, London SE11 5AY. Tel: 020 7640 0042. © 2023 The Incorporated Catholic Truth Society. www.ctsbooks.org

ISBN: 978 1 78469 755 6

Contents

The Eucharist, the sacrament of our salvation accomplished by Christ on the cross,…is the making present…of his unique sacrifice, in the liturgy of the Church, which is his Body.

Catechism of the Catholic Church (CCC) 1359, 1362

Introduction

It has been my experience over a period of thirty-five years as a religion teacher and catechist, in the UK and abroad, that the average baptised Catholic is not aware of the amazing fact that when we attend Mass we are actually present at Calvary. Perhaps this is why one of the titles for the Mass, 'the Holy Sacrifice of the Mass', is not familiar to many Catholics today.

The aim of this booklet is to shine a light on this reality, engendering in the reader awe and wonder at the extraordinary event that takes place at every Mass – which, it is hoped, will in turn lead to adoration, praise and thanksgiving to our Father God, who sent his Son Jesus Christ to be "the sacrifice that takes our sins away, and not only ours, but the whole world's" (*1 Jn* 2:2).

A conscious awareness that at each celebration of Mass we are truly present at the foot of the cross, offering ourselves with Jesus to the Father, should lead us to experience an entirely different attitude and atmosphere than if we were attending, say, a mere memorial service or community gathering. Let us ask the Holy Spirit himself to enlighten us through the holy Scriptures and the teaching of the Church presented in this booklet.

Why the Mass Is Called a "Holy Sacrifice"

The Holy Sacrifice of the Mass is the *same sacrifice* as that of Jesus on the cross at Calvary, "a real event that occurred in our history, but it is *unique*: all other historical events happen once, and then they pass away, swallowed up in the past. The Paschal Mystery of Christ, by contrast, cannot remain only in the past, because…[Christ] participates in the *divine eternity*, and so *transcends all times while being made present in them all*" (*CCC* 1085, author's emphasis).

The Son of God is both *fully man* and *fully God*: he has a human nature and a divine nature. As man, Jesus Christ lived in *time,* at a particular moment in history. *Time* is a creation of God: there was a beginning of time and there will be an end of time.

But because the Son of God is divine, he is *eternal – without beginning or end,* the "*Everlasting Now*". So, *Time* and *Eternity* meet in the Person of Jesus Christ – which is why we are able to *be actually present* at the foot of the cross on Calvary at every Mass.

It is also why it was possible for Christ to offer his one and only sacrifice *for all human beings*: "There is not, never has been, and never will be a single human being for whom Christ did not suffer" (*CCC* 605).

This truth of our faith is referred to by the Church as a "mystery", which does not mean something obscure or unreasonable. On the contrary, the theological definition of "mystery" is: "religious truth divinely revealed, especially one beyond human reason" (*The Concise Oxford Dictionary*). According to the *Catechism*,

> The sacrifice of Christ and the sacrifice of the Eucharist are *one single sacrifice*: "The victim is one and the same: the same now offers through the ministry of priests, who then offered himself on the cross; only the manner of offering is different." "And since in this divine sacrifice which is celebrated in the Mass, the same Christ who offered himself once in a bloody manner on the altar of the cross is contained and is offered in an un-bloody manner…this sacrifice is truly propitiatory." (*CCC* 1367)

You may ask, "But don't we hear in the Mass the words, 'Do this in memory of me'?" Yes, we do. In the context of the Eucharistic celebration, the word "memory", or "remembrance", rests on the Hebrew root word "*zkr*", which, in Judaism and the Old Testament, means *making present the past so that it can be effective in the present*. For the early Fathers of the Church, it meant bringing before the Father the one, complete sacrifice of his Son Jesus Christ, so that its power is experienced and effective within the Eucharist and thus received by those present.

The Mystery of the Mass

Let us continue with two more definitions of the word "mystery" in a theological context:

- *mystery*: any religious truth known to man only through divine revelation (*Webster's New World Dictionary*).

- *mystery*: any truth that is divinely revealed but otherwise unknowable (*Collins English Dictionary*).

The following example from Sacred Scripture and later Church teachings might help to clarify these definitions:

When Jesus came to the region of Caesarea Philippi, he asked his disciples, "Who do people say the Son of Man is?" And they said, "Some say he is John the Baptist, some Elijah, and others Jeremiah or one of the prophets." "But you," he said, "who do you say that I am?" Then Simon Peter spoke up, "You are the Christ," he said, "the Son of the living God." Jesus replied, "Simon son of Jonah, you are a happy man! Because *it was not flesh and blood that revealed this to you but my Father in heaven*." (*Mt* 16:13-17, author's emphasis)

The Church tells us:

- "Through divine revelation, God chose to show forth and communicate *himself* and the eternal decisions of his will regarding the salvation of men. That is to say, he chose to share with them those divine treasures which totally transcend the understanding of the human mind." (*Dei Verbum* 6, author's emphasis)

- "Of all visible creatures, only man is 'able to know and love his creator'. He is the only creature on earth that God willed for its own sake, and he alone is called to share, by knowledge and love, in God's own life. It was for this end that he was created, and this is the fundamental reason for his dignity." (*CCC* 356)

- "God himself is an eternal exchange of love, Father, Son and Holy Spirit, and he has destined us to share in that exchange."(*CCC* 221)

God created us so that we can know him, not merely know about him! It is a great shame that there is only one word for "know" in the English language. Other languages, such as French and Spanish, have two. The French use the verbs *savoir* and *connaître*, the former meaning to know facts or information, the latter referring to a personal familiarity, to "know by experience". In Spanish, the distinctive words for "know" are *saber* and *conocer*. *Saber* is used in the context of knowing information or ideas, while *conocer* –

"to be familiar with" – is used in the context of personally knowing a person or a place.

Knowing God

Faith in God does not merely refer to knowing truths *about* him, it also includes knowing him *through his revelation of himself*, experiencing his extraordinary personal love for us. He wants a relationship of familiarity with us, which he initiates and we respond to. In his Apostolic Letter *Desiderio Desideravi* (*DD*), Pope Francis reminds us:

> We may not even be aware of it, but every time we go to Mass, the first reason is that we are drawn there by His desire for us… For our part, the possible response… is, as always, that surrender to this love, that letting ourselves be drawn by Him. (*DD* 6)

St Augustine spent his youth searching for truth, but after his encounter with Christ, he wrote in his *Confessions*, "You have made us for yourself, O Lord, and our hearts are restless until they rest in You."

> Man's faculties make him capable of coming to a knowledge of the existence of a personal God. But for man to be able to enter into real intimacy with him, God willed to both reveal himself to man and to give him the grace of being able to welcome this revelation in faith. (*CCC* 35)

Pope Benedict XVI explained that "faith does not just mean accepting a certain number of abstract truths… Faith consists in an intimate relationship with Christ".[1]

St John Paul II declared that "faith…is neither an abstract discourse nor a vague religious sentiment, but a personal encounter with Christ who gives new meaning to life".[2] Speaking to the European bishops, he insisted that: "Without the vibrance of this encounter, Christianity becomes a soulless religious traditionalism which easily yields to the attacks of secularism or the enticements of alternative religious offerings".[3]

The assistance of the Holy Spirit is essential

In his encyclical on the Holy Spirit, Pope John Paul II gave a wonderfully helpful definition of faith: "Faith, in its deepest essence, is the openness of the human heart to the gift: to God's self-communication in the Holy Spirit."[4] "Heart" here is meant "in the biblical sense of the depths of one's being, where the person decides for or against God" (*CCC* 368). We need to ask the Holy Spirit to help us to open our hearts to him:

---

[1] Pope Benedict XVI, Homily in Poland, 26th May 2006.

[2] Pope John Paul II, *L'Osservatore Romano*, p.7, 20th February 2003.

[3] Pope John Paul II, *Ad Limina* visit of Lithuanian Bishops, *L'Osservatore Romano*, p.8, 27th September 1999.

[4] Pope John Paul II, *Dominum et Vivificantem* 51.

Faith is a gift of God, a supernatural virtue infused by him. "Before this faith can be exercised, man must have the grace of God to move and assist him; he must have the interior helps of the Holy Spirit, who moves the heart and converts it to God, who opens the eyes of the mind and makes it easy for all to accept and believe the truth." (*CCC* 153)[5]

Catholic teaching has always recognised two aspects to faith, which it distinguishes by the terms *fides quae* (objective revealed truth given by God through Sacred Scripture and the Church's teaching Tradition) and *fides qua* (the personal surrender and commitment to God inspired in us by the Holy Spirit). Clearly, both aspects of faith are essential to our lives as Catholics, but without *fides qua* our faith remains lifeless and impersonal.[6]

The encounter with Christ

We comprehend mystery when we encounter the Risen Jesus. "Only the action of the Spirit can bring to completion our knowledge of the mystery of God, for the mystery of God is not something grasped mentally but a relationship that touches all of life. Such experience is fundamental" (*DD* 39).

---

[5] *CCC* 153 cites *Dei Verbum* 5.
[6] See Gerald O'Collins and Edward G. Farrugia, *A Concise Dictionary of Theology* (Edinburgh: T&T Clark, 1991), 75.

When we experience a living intimacy with the Lord, we find that at Mass "every gesture and every word…is always new because it meets with an always new moment in our lives" (*DD* 53). Mass can never be boring!

There are times when I have inwardly gasped at the words the priest says as he adds a drop of water to the wine in the chalice: "By the mystery of this water and wine *may we come to share in the divinity of Christ who humbled himself to share in our humanity.*" The momentousness of that reality is so awesome that one almost needs a time of silence to respond with heartfelt gratitude and joy.

Since God created us to know him personally and to respond to his love, this means that it is possible, and necessary, to encounter Christ Jesus. Many are afraid of an encounter with Jesus because they intuit that their lives would inevitably change. Even though the Lord says in both the Old and the New Testaments that "you must love the Lord your God with all your heart, with all your soul, and with all your mind" (*Dt* 6:4-5; *Mt* 22:37), they fear being perceived by others as a "fanatic".

Pope Benedict XVI addressed these fears in his first homily as Pope:

Are we not perhaps all afraid in some way? If we let Christ enter fully into our lives, if we open ourselves totally to him, are we not afraid that he might take something away from us? Are we not perhaps afraid to give up something significant, something unique, something that makes life so beautiful? Do we not then risk ending up diminished and deprived of our freedom? No! If we let Christ into our lives, we lose nothing, nothing, absolutely nothing of what makes life free, beautiful and great. No! Only in this friendship are the doors of life opened wide. Only in this friendship is the great potential of human existence truly revealed. Only in this friendship do we experience beauty and liberation.

And so, today, with great strength and great conviction, on the basis of long personal experience of life, I say to you, dear young people: Do not be afraid of Christ! He takes nothing away and he gives you everything. When we give ourselves to him, we receive a hundredfold in return. Yes, open, open wide the doors to Christ – and you will find true life. Amen.

Pope John Paul II began his ministry with a similar proclamation: "Do not be afraid! Open wide the doors for Christ!"

In his first encyclical, Pope Francis invited "all Christians, everywhere, at this very moment, to a renewed personal encounter with Jesus Christ, or at least an openness to letting him encounter them". He exhorted:

I ask all of you to do this unfailingly each day. No one should think that this invitation is not meant for him or her, since "no one is excluded from the joy brought by the Lord". The Lord does not disappoint those who take this risk; whenever we take a step towards Jesus, we come to realise that he is already there, waiting for us with open arms. (*Evangelii Gaudium* 3)

The liturgy: place of encounter with Christ

Referring to the Mass, Pope St Paul VI declared: "The liturgy is the first source of *divine communion* in which God shares his own life with us" (cited in *DD* 30).[7] When the Word of God is proclaimed, it is Christ himself who is speaking to us. When we receive Holy Communion, we are receiving the Risen Christ, as Pope Francis explains:

Here lies the powerful beauty of the liturgy. If the resurrection were for us a concept, an idea, a thought; if the Risen One were for us the recollection of the recollection of others, however authoritative, as for example, of the Apostles; if there were not given also to us the possibility of a true encounter with him, that would be to declare the newness of the Word made flesh to have been all used up. Instead, the Incarnation, in addition to being the only always new event that history knows, is also the very method that the Holy Trinity has chosen to open to us the way of communion. Christian faith is either an encounter with him alive, or it does not exist. The Liturgy guarantees for us the possibility of such an encounter. (*DD* 10, 11)

---

[7] AAS 56 (1964) 34.

Pope Francis continues:

> It becomes clear that knowledge of *the mystery of Christ*, the decisive question for our lives, does not consist in a mental assimilation of some idea but in real…engagement with his person. In this sense *Liturgy* is not about "knowledge"… The celebration concerns *the reality of our being docile to the Spirit who operates through it until Christ be formed in us* (cf. *Ga* 4:19)… This is the purpose for which the Spirit is given, whose action is always and only to confect the Body of Christ. (*DD* 41, author's emphasis)

Why Did Jesus Die for You?

Growing up as a Catholic I had always been taught that Jesus died on the cross for my sins, but as I got older I wondered why his terrible suffering and death were necessary for my personal sins, which I knew I needed to confess, but which were certainly not on the same scale as those of someone like Hitler.

It was not until I attended a retreat in my early thirties that the penny dropped. The Holy Spirit revealed the Person of Jesus Christ to me, which was altogether different from learning about him in religion classes, important as that was.

The Holy Spirit is sent to "witness to Jesus" (see *Jn* 15:26), and he does so in a way that surpasses our natural understanding. Since he is spirit, he speaks to our innermost being, our spirit, Person to person. The Holy Spirit opens our minds to comprehend Christ's death and Resurrection: "He makes present the mystery of Christ" (*CCC* 737).

The understanding that the Holy Spirit gives of the death of Christ on the cross includes a realisation of our own sin, but amazingly, the Holy Spirit does it in such a way that, at the very same time, we experience his consoling love. This is what is called "the light of divine Revelation".

Only the light of divine Revelation clarifies the reality of sin… Without the knowledge Revelation gives of God we cannot recognise sin clearly and are tempted to explain it as merely a developmental flaw, a psychological weakness, a mistake, or the necessary consequence of an inadequate social structure, etc. (*CCC* 387)

What is sin?

Sin is a refusal to hear the word of God: "Quite frequently in both the Old and in the New Testament, we find sin described as a *refusal to hear the word*…and thus as being closed to God who calls us to communion with himself" (Benedict XVI, *Verbum Domini* 26). Primarily, sin is about man's relationship to God, his creator:

> To try to understand what sin is, one must first recognise the profound relation of man to God, for only in this relationship is the evil of sin unmasked in its true identity as humanity's rejection of God and opposition to him. (*CCC* 386)

We need to go back to man's beginning, to the first book of the Bible, Genesis, which describes the creation of the first human beings and their relationship to God.

The origin of sin

God has revealed himself as a Trinity of Persons: Father, Son and Holy Spirit. The trinitarian God created us in his image and likeness. In Genesis, we read that God said, "Let us make man in our image, in the likeness of ourselves" (1:26), so we, too, are "trinitarian": spirit, soul and body, as Pope Benedict XVI explained, quoting Scripture:

> "May the God of peace himself", St Paul writes, "sanctify you wholly; and may your spirit and soul and body be kept sound and blameless for the coming of our Lord Jesus Christ" (*1 Th* 5:23). We are, therefore, spirit, soul and body. We are part of this world, tied to the possibilities and limitations of our material condition, while at the same time we are open to an infinite horizon, able to converse with God and to welcome him within us.[8]

The Church teaches that our first parents, Adam and Eve, shared in God's divine life: they were in a state of "original holiness" because God is holy. "The first man was not only created good, but was also established in friendship with his Creator and in harmony with himself and with the creation around him" (*CCC* 374).

Since they were in the image of God's own nature, they were therefore "imperishable" – *immortal* (see *Ws* 2:23). As long as they remained in the "divine intimacy" of communion with God, they would never suffer or die (see *CCC* 376).

---

[8] Pope Benedict XVI, Homily, Vespers 27th September 2010.

Obviously, this description of human beings in the state of "original holiness" and living forever is not what human beings experience now. So what happened to change all of that? Using what St John Paul II referred to as a "symbolic narrative", Sacred Scripture tells us about the separation of man from his life of union with God through the story of Adam and Eve in the Garden of Eden: "The account of the Fall in Genesis 3 uses figurative language but affirms a primeval event, a deed that took place *at the beginning of the history of man*" (*CCC* 390).

The story tells us that God in his perfect love placed our first parents in the Garden of Eden, a paradise. God told them they could eat from any of the trees in the Garden except the tree of knowledge of good and bad: "From that tree you shall not eat; the moment you eat from it you are surely doomed to die" (*Gn* 2:17).

What was God telling them? All the treasures of wisdom and knowledge are in God (*Col* 2:3) who shared his entire being with his children, Adam and Eve. The Church has always taught that the Second Person of the Blessed Trinity is Wisdom personified, which Jesus himself confirmed when he identified himself as the Truth (see *Jn* 14:6). If Adam and Eve chose to seek "wisdom" apart from Wisdom himself, they would be separating themselves from God, who is also *eternal life*. In other words, they would *die*. God was merely warning them of the consequences of such a choice.

The figurative language in the story of Adam and Eve in the Garden shows the devil as a serpent:

> The serpent said to the woman, "You certainly will not die!"…The woman saw that the tree was…desirable for gaining wisdom. So she took some of its fruit and ate it; and she also gave some to her husband, who was with her, and he ate it. (*Gn* 3:4, 6)

We know from Scripture and the teaching of the Church that the devil is the archangel Lucifer, who was created good by God but who rebelled against him, was thrown down to earth and "deceived the whole world" (*Rv* 12:9). Jesus called the devil "the father of lies" and "a murderer from the beginning" (*Jn* 8:44-45).

By their choice to disobey God's word and believe the lie of the evil one, our first parents consciously separated themselves from God, their source of love, holiness, wisdom and eternal life. This separation is referred to as "the Fall" – man's fall from *grace*: "Grace is a participation in the life of God" (*CCC* 1997). Pope St Paul VI explained that the devil is "the wily, fatal tempter involved in the first sin, the original sin [which was] the profound *cause of death* because it involved *detachment from God, the source of life*."[9]

Man, tempted by the devil, let his trust in his Creator die in his heart and, abusing his freedom, *disobeyed* God's

---

[9] Pope Paul VI, General Audience, 15th November 1972.

command. This is what man's first sin consisted of. All subsequent sin would be disobedience towards God and lack of trust in his goodness. (*CCC* 397)

In that sin, man *preferred* himself to God and by that very act scorned him. He chose himself over and against God, and against the requirements of his creaturely status and therefore against his own good. Created in a state of holiness, man was destined to be fully "divinised" by God in glory. Seduced by the devil, he wanted to "be like God", but "without God, before God, and not in accordance with God". (*CCC* 398)

By our first parents' sin, the devil acquired a certain domination over man, even though man remains free. Original sin entails "captivity under the power of him who thenceforth had the power of death, that is, the devil." (*CCC* 407)

The fatal consequences of sin

The *Catechism* describes how "Scripture portrays the tragic consequences of this first disobedience":

1. Adam and Eve…lose the grace of original holiness.

2. They become afraid of the God of whom they have conceived a distorted image…

3. The harmony in which they had found themselves, thanks to original justice, is now destroyed.

4. The control of the soul's spiritual faculties over the body is shattered.

5. The union of man and woman becomes subject to tensions, their relations henceforth marked by lust and domination.

6. Harmony with creation is broken: visible creation has become alien and hostile to man.

7. Because of man, creation is now subject "to its bondage to decay".

8. Finally, the consequence explicitly foretold for this disobedience will come true... *Death makes its entrance into human history.* (*CCC* 399, 400)

"Disfigured by sin and death, man remains 'in the *image* of God'...but is deprived 'of the glory of God', of his '*likeness*'...the Spirit who is 'the giver of life'" (*CCC* 705, author's emphasis).

Without the life-giving Spirit of God dwelling within them, fallen human beings are spiritually dead. Since they are no longer in union with Wisdom himself, "Intellectually they are in the dark, and they are estranged from the life of God" (*Ep* 14:18). Therefore, "Sin brought man to a lower state, forcing him away from the completeness that is his to attain" (*Gaudium et Spes* 13). Every human being is born in this state.

"How did the sin of Adam become the sin of all his descendants?..."By yielding to the tempter, Adam and

Eve committed a *personal sin*, but this sin affected *the human nature* they would then transmit *in a fallen state …* a human nature deprived of original holiness" (*CCC* 404).

The late Fr Ian Petit, OSB, addressed this unfortunate human condition:

> That there is something wrong with human nature is fairly obvious: the good we plan to do often ends in failure. We like to blame this on the star we were born under, or on the fact that our mother made a negative remark to us. We resist admitting that the fault may lie within us, and much time is spent searching for a cause, hoping we can find a remedy. Today many courses are offered to help us look into the mystery of ourselves and some of our peculiarities. These may have value in aiding our understanding of why we do this or feel that, but the trouble is that the various wounds we may have received in childhood are not the real cause for our behaviour, for long before these wounds happened we were already wounded. These hurts have only added to the trouble already there. … The story of the Fall is not to be taken literally … What we are being told is that Satan tempted Eve to live by her own intelligence rather than by what God said. She was being tempted to live independently from God. The fact that she obeyed has radically wounded human nature.[10]

---

[10] Raniero Cantalamessa, OFM cap and Ian Petit, OSB, *Another Gospel? Current Theories and Practices which Obscure the Good News* (Proclaim Publications).

When, by God's grace, I grasped the reality of the human condition, I realised that, just like every other human being, I too needed to be restored to God's original plan for human beings, to be fully human as God intended. So the question is: "How can the fallen human being free himself from his sinful condition, from death and the domination of the devil, and be restored to union with Eternal Life himself?" The answer is that he cannot. God himself had to rescue us.

Be Reconciled to God

God so loved the world so much that he gave his only Son, so that everyone who believes in him might not be lost but might have eternal life.

(*Jn* 3:16)

The "Paschal Mystery" of Christ refers to *God's plan of salvation for all humanity* which was fulfilled through the Passion, death, Resurrection, and Ascension of Jesus Christ.

Jesus means in Hebrew "God saves". At the annunciation, the angel Gabriel gave him the name Jesus as his proper name, which expresses both his identity and his mission. Since God alone can forgive sins, it is God who, in Jesus his eternal Son made man, "will save his people from their sins". (*CCC* 430)

Jesus is the Word of God through whom everything was created (see *Jn* 1:1-3; *Col* 1:15-17). Since everything was created through the Word of God, everything had to be restored through the Word of God. It was man who, tempted by the devil, chose to separate himself from

God; so Jesus had to become man to "take on the whole weakness of our lowly human nature" in order to restore us to union with God. Pope St Leo the Great explains why Jesus had to take on our fallen human nature:

> If he who was alone free from sin had not united our nature to himself, then men would have still been held captive under the power of the devil. We would have been incapable of profiting by the Victor's triumph if the battle had been fought outside our nature. (Pope St Leo the Great, PL 54, 791-793)

Pope St Leo the Great

The Son of God who was in the beginning with God, through whom all things were made, without whom nothing was made [(*Jn* 1)], became man to free him from eternal death.

He stooped down to take up our lowliness without loss to his own glory. He remained what he was; he took up what he was not. He wanted to join the very nature of a servant to that nature in which he is equal to God the Father. He wanted to unite both natures in an alliance so wonderful that the glory of the greater would not annihilate the lesser, nor the taking up of the lower diminish the greatness of the higher.

What belongs to each nature is preserved intact and meets the other in one person: lowliness is taken up by greatness, weakness by power, mortality by eternity. To pay the debt of our human condition, a nature incapable of suffering is united to a nature capable of suffering, and true God and true man are forged into the unity that is the Lord. This was done to make possible the kind of remedy that fitted our human need: one and the same mediator between God and men able to die because of one nature, able to rise again because of the other.

(*Sermo* 1, *In Navitate Domini*)

Jesus lived his entire human life obeying the word of his Father. When he died on the cross, our fallen human nature died. Because Jesus Christ is also the immortal God, his mortal body rose from the dead. On the cross, Jesus conquered sin, Satan and death: "By his death, Christ liberates us from sin; by his Resurrection, he opens for us the way to a new life. This new life…reinstates us in God's grace" (*CCC* 654).

Jesus is called the "new Adam" because he initiated a new creation who will no longer die. Anyone who is born spiritually as a new creation in Christ through faith and baptism, and who remains in union with him, will live forever, just as God intended in the beginning.

The Church warns us that "this new life as a child of God can be weakened and even lost by sin" (*CCC* 1420). The new life in Christ is experienced when we choose to live "no longer for ourselves but for him who died and rose again for us" (Eucharistic Prayer IV). Jesus said: "If anyone wants to be a follower of mine, let him renounce himself and take up his cross every day and follow me" (*Lk* 9:23).

To renounce someone is to disown him. To renounce oneself is to disown *oneself* as *the centre of one's existence*, which is the condition of the fallen human being, referred to in Scripture as the *natural man,* the *unspiritual man,* or man *in the flesh.* Pope Benedict XVI explained what these terms indicate: "a way of living only for oneself and according to worldly standards".[11]

Living only for oneself means that our own ideas, opinions, judgements and preferences are at the centre, rather than Jesus Christ, the Way, the Truth and the Life.

Living according to worldly standards means that our temporal, secular life and its concerns and pursuits are more important to us than the Kingdom of God and our baptismal vocation as disciples of Jesus.

Remaining in union with God

Once we have been baptised – immersed in God's life and freed from the power of the evil one (the Sacrament of

---

[11] Pope Benedict XVI, address to students and teachers of the ecclesiastical universities of Rome on 30th October 2008.

Baptism includes an exorcism) – we need to live our new life *in the Spirit*, not in the flesh:

> Let me put it like this; if you are guided by the Spirit you will be in no danger of yielding to self-indulgence, since self-indulgence is the opposite of the Spirit, the Spirit is totally against such a thing, and it is precisely because the two are so opposed that you do not always carry out your good intentions. (*Ga* 5:16-17)

To live as new creations in Christ we need to be made more and more like him. The word of God encourages us to "die" to our old self – our fallen nature – and put on the new self:

> You must give up your old way of life; you must put aside your old self, which gets corrupted by following illusory desires. Your mind must be renewed by a spiritual revolution so that you can put on the new self that has been created in God's way, in the goodness and holiness of the truth. (*Ep* 4:22-24)

Scripture gives us specific instructions as to what that entails (e.g. *Ep* 4:24-6:17). Since the word of God is a living word, it is effective if we are open to receive it:

> The word of God is something alive and active: it cuts like any double-edged sword but more finely: it can slip through the place where the soul is divided from the

spirit, or joints from the marrow; it can judge the secret emotions and thoughts. (*Heb* 4:12)

When we nourish ourselves with the word of God, "this nourishment enlightens the mind, strengthens the will and fires the hearts of men and women with the love of God" (*Dei Verbum* 23).

In the liturgy, we are fed at both the table of the word and the table of the Eucharist:

The Risen Lord is encountered in the Sunday assembly at the twofold table of the word and of the Bread of Life. ... [I]t is Christ who speaks, present as he is in his word "when Sacred Scripture is read in the Church". (Pope St John Paul II, *Dies Domini* 39)

We must ask for the grace to respond to him.

The Mass: The Sacred Liturgy

The liturgy "is the gift of the Paschal Mystery of the Lord which, received with docility, makes our life new" (Pope Francis, *DD* 20). We were made new creations in Christ at baptism, and we are more and more united with him through the Eucharist:

> The celebration of the Eucharistic sacrifice is wholly directed toward the intimate union of the faithful with Christ through communion. To receive communion is to receive Christ himself who has offered himself for us. (*CCC* 1382)

> The Lord addresses an invitation to us, urging us to receive him in the sacrament of the Eucharist: 'Truly, I say to you, unless you eat the flesh of the Son of man and drink his blood, you have no life in you.' (*CCC* 1384)

"These words of the Lord reawaken in us our amazement for the gift of the Eucharist. No one in the world, as much they might love another person, can make themselves become food for them. God did so, and does so, for us" (Pope Francis).[12]

---

[12] Pope Francis, *Angelus*, 8th August 2022.

In his encyclical *Laudato Si*, Pope Francis wrote:

It is in the Eucharist that all that has been created finds its greatest exaltation. Grace, which tends to manifest itself tangibly, found unsurpassable expression when God Himself became man and gave Himself as food for His creatures. The Lord, in the culmination of the mystery of the Incarnation, chose to reach our intimate depths through a fragment of matter. (236)

With a joyful urgency, Pope Francis exhorts us to be aware of the great gifts the Lord offers us at every Mass:

We need to be present at that [Last] Supper, to be able to hear his voice, to eat his Body and to drink his Blood. We need him. In the Eucharist and in all the sacraments we are guaranteed the possibility of encountering the Lord Jesus and of having the power of his Paschal Mystery reach us. The salvific power of the sacrifice of Jesus. (*DD* 11)

St Francis of Assisi

Let everyone be struck with fear,
let the whole world tremble,
and let the heavens exult when Christ,
the Son of the living God,
is present on the altar in the hands of a priest!
O wonderful loftiness and stupendous dignity!

O sublime humility! O humble sublimity!
The Lord of the universe, God and the Son of God,
so humbles Himself that for our salvation
He hides Himself under an ordinary piece of bread!
Brothers, look at the humility of God,
and pour out your hearts before Him!
Humble yourselves that you may be exalted by Him!
Hold back nothing of yourselves for yourselves,
that He Who gives Himself totally to you
may receive you totally!

Preparing for the sacred liturgy

"Every eighth day the Church celebrates in the Lord's day
the event of our salvation. Sunday…is a gift that God makes
for his people; and for this reason the Church safeguards it
with a precept" (*DD* 65). What is that 'precept'?

The precept of the Church specifies: "On Sundays and
other holy days of obligation the faithful are bound to
participate in the Mass"…unless excused for a serious
reason (for example: illness, the care of infants). Those
who deliberately fail in this obligation commit a grave
sin. (*CCC* 2180, 2181)

Many years ago, I lived on a small Caribbean island,
where I was involved in our little parish. One day a couple

came for baptism preparation, which is required by the Church before the Sacrament of Baptism can be conferred on their child. I had never seen them at Mass, and our bishop, who lived on a larger island, had made it clear that those coming for the sacraments needed to be practising their Catholic faith. I asked the baby's mother, "When he was born, did you feed your baby only once, or have you continued feeding him since his birth?" Obviously her answer was that she had continued feeding her baby. So I explained that in baptism we are *born spiritually* – we receive a new life in Christ Jesus – and that new *spiritual life* also needs continual feeding and nurturing or we will die spiritually, just as we would die physically without corporal nourishment.

This is why Holy Mother Church safeguards with a precept the necessity of attending Sunday Mass and explains why "those who deliberately fail in this obligation commit a grave sin". For this reason, "We must *prepare ourselves* for so great and so holy a moment. St Paul urges us to examine our conscience... Anyone conscious of a grave sin must receive the sacrament of Reconciliation before coming to communion" (*CCC* 1385).

Holy Mother Church addresses all of us who come to the liturgical assembly:

The assembly should *prepare* itself to encounter its Lord and become "a people well disposed". The preparation of hearts is the joint work of the Holy Spirit and the assembly, especially of its ministers. The grace of the Holy Spirit seeks to awaken faith, conversion of heart, and adherence to the Father's will. These dispositions are the precondition both for the reception of other graces conferred in the celebration itself and the fruits of new life which the celebration is intended to produce afterwards." (*CCC* 1098)

Eucharistic Adoration

Jesus Christ is present in the sacred liturgy and he remains present – body, blood, soul and divinity – in the consecrated host, in which he resides in every tabernacle in the world. There he awaits us, our Lord and Saviour, looking forward to a visit from those he has rescued from eternal death and to whom he offers eternal life with him: "I have come so that they may have life and have it to the full" (*Jn* 10:10).

We should always acknowledge the presence of our Lord in the tabernacle whenever we enter a Catholic church. "In the liturgy of the Mass we express our faith in the real presence of Christ under the species of bread and wine by, among other ways, genuflecting or bowing deeply as a sign of adoration of the Lord" (*CCC* 1378).

I recall that there was a Pew survey a few years ago which claimed that 70 per cent of US Catholics do not believe in the real presence of Jesus Christ in the Eucharist. This unbelief has always cropped up in the Church and has sometimes been a catalyst for a miraculous intervention. Take the first known incidence of a Eucharistic miracle – in Lanciano, Italy, in the eighth century: a monk celebrating Mass had doubts about the real presence of Jesus Christ, and after saying the words of consecration over the bread and wine, the host was changed into living flesh and the wine was changed into real blood, which can still be seen today. Over the centuries, various scientific investigations have taken place which have concluded that both the flesh and the blood are human, the flesh being muscular tissue of the heart, the blood type AB. Many other Eucharistic miracles have occurred since then in various countries.

Why is it that even people who have been baptised have such trouble believing supernatural realities? After Jesus died and rose from the dead, he admonished his unbelieving disciples:

Having risen in the morning on the first day of the week, he appeared first to Mary of Magdala from whom he had cast out seven devils. She then went to those who had been his companions, and who were mourning and in tears, and told them. But they did not believe her when they heard her say that he was alive and that she had seen him. After this, he showed himself under another form to two of them as they were on their way into the country. These went back and told the others, who did not believe him either. Lastly, he showed himself to the Eleven themselves while they were at table. He reproached them for their incredulity and obstinacy, because they had refused to believe those who had seen him after he had risen. (*Mk* 16:9-14)

These disciples of Jesus, especially the Apostles, had personally spent three years with Jesus, listening to his words, witnessing his miracles, enjoying his friendship. Pope Benedict XVI gave us some insight into their lack of genuine faith:

> Knowing "from a human point of view"…means knowing solely in an external way, by means of external criteria… [Jesus] asked the Apostles…"Who do you say that I am?" The people know him, but superficially; they know various things about him, but they do not really know him.[13]

Scripture speaks about the distinction between the "natural man" and the "spiritual man": "An unspiritual person is one who does not accept anything of the Spirit of God: he sees it all as nonsense; it is beyond his understanding because it can only be understood by means of the Spirit" (*1 Co* 2:14). A footnote in my *New American Bible* explains this situation:

> *Spiritual people…fleshly people*: Paul employs two clusters of concepts and terms to distinguish what later theology will call the "natural" and the "supernatural". The natural person is one whose existence, perceptions, and behaviour are determined by purely natural principles… Such persons are only infants; they remain

---

[13] Pope Benedict XVI, General Audience, 8th October 2008.

on a purely human level. On the other hand, they are called to be animated by a higher principle…God's Spirit. They are to become spiritual and mature in their perceptions and behaviour. (*NAB*, *1 Co* 3:1)

Just before his Ascension to heaven, Jesus told the Apostles "not to leave Jerusalem, but to wait there for what the Father had promised. 'It is' he had said 'what you have heard me speak about: John baptised with water but you, not many days from now, will be baptised with the Holy Spirit'" (*Acts* 1:4-5). The Apostles, along with Mary and some other disciples, experienced the outpouring of the Holy Spirit at Pentecost.

In his book *The Lord,* Romano Guardini writes:

Before Pentecost the disciples had lived "in the sight" of Christ; now they lived *in* him; before they had spoken about him; now they spoke *through* him. In the Holy Spirit, man shares in Christ's existence… The vital exchange between God and man established on that first Pentecost continues throughout time. This does not mean that man merely thinks of Christ or lovingly cherishes his image; what exists in him is the living reality of Jesus.

The Holy Spirit, the third Person of the Blessed Trinity, is the Love between the Father and the Son personified. The *Catechism* teaches us:

1. "One cannot believe in Jesus Christ without sharing in his Spirit. It is the Holy Spirit who reveals to men who Jesus is." (152)

2. "This knowledge of faith is possible only in the Holy Spirit: to be in touch with Christ, we must first have been touched by the Holy Spirit." (683)

3. "Every time we begin to pray to Jesus it is the Holy Spirit who draws us on the way of prayer by his prevenient grace." (2670)

COME, HOLY SPIRIT!

Fill the hearts of your faithful,
and enkindle in us the fire of your love!

Adoration of Jesus Christ in the Blessed Sacrament

The *Catechism*, citing Pope St Paul VI, encourages us to make frequent visits to worship the Blessed Sacrament in the tabernacle:

Because Christ himself is present in the sacrament of the altar, he is to be honoured with the worship of adoration. "To visit the Blessed Sacrament is…a proof of gratitude, an expression of love, and a duty of adoration toward Christ our Lord" (*CCC* 1418, citing Paul VI, *Mysterium Fidei* 66).

And according to Pope St John Paul II:

> The Church and the world have a great need for Eucharistic worship. Jesus awaits us in this sacrament of love. Let us not refuse the time to go to meet him in adoration, in contemplation full of faith, and open to making amends for the serious offences and crimes of the world. Let our adoration never cease."
> (*Dominicae Cenae* 3)

Pope Francis recommends time spent in prayer and silent adoration to better come to know the Lord:

> Every Christian who is not afraid to devote time to prayer can make his or her own the words of the Apostle Paul, who says this: "the life I now live in the flesh I live by faith in the Son of God, who loved me and gave himself for me" (*Ga* 2:20). Prayer makes you aware of this. Only in the silence of adoration do we experience the whole truth of these words. And we must recapture this sense of adoration. To adore, to adore God, to adore Jesus, to adore the Spirit. The Father, the Son and the Spirit: to adore. In silence. The prayer of adoration is that prayer that makes us recognise God as the beginning and the end of all of History. And this prayer is the living flame of the Spirit that gives strength to witness and to mission.[14]

---

[14] Pope Francis, General Audience, 25th November 2020.

Epilogue: Reflections on the Encounter with Jesus

Reflections on first encounters with Jesus

"When you first were aware of encountering Jesus, in what way did that encounter happen?"

These are some of the responses I have been offered when I have asked this question:

RESPONSE 1

I was deeply touched by someone whom I observed behaving in a Christlike way. It was a graced moment which drew my mind and heart towards the Lord.

For reflection: Would you say this was an encounter with Jesus himself which resulted in a new or renewed personal relationship with him?

RESPONSE 2

I experienced a profound awareness of God while observing a sunset [or another beautiful phenomenon of nature]. It seemed to be a very spiritual moment.

For reflection: Scripture tells us that what can be known about God is evident because his invisible attributes of eternal power and divinity have been able to be understood and perceived through his creation: "Ever since God created the world his everlasting power and deity – however invisible – have been there for the mind to see in the things he has made." (*Rm* 1:20)

If we move one step further from a revelation about God's attributes through experiencing his creation to seeking the One through whom all creation came to be – Jesus (see *Jn* 1:1-3) – we will encounter him.

RESPONSE 3

When I began to study the teachings of the Church I was totally captivated and knew within my whole being that this was the truth. So I would say that – since Jesus is the Truth – I know Jesus because I know those truths.

For reflection: "This is the testimony: God has given us eternal life, and this life is in his Son; anyone who has the Son has life, anyone who does not have the Son does not have life" (*1 Jn* 5:11-12). As important as the teachings of the Church are, we cannot have a relationship with a doctrine. One biblical footnote explains: "To possess the Son is not acceptance of a doctrine but of a person who lives now and provides life" (*New American Bible*, *1 Jn* 5:11-12).

RESPONSE 4

After saying a prayer of repentance and asking God's forgiveness for living a "self-designed life" instead of following him, I experienced Jesus himself within *me* (*which was a shock, because previously it had always seemed that he was "outside" me – and rather far away!*) *I was immersed in deep peace and filled with his love for me personally.*

For reflection: Has this encounter transformed your life?

Reflections on the fruits of an encounter with Jesus

Pope Francis: [*V*]*ery simply: the joy of the Gospel springs from the encounter with Jesus. It is when we encounter the Lord that we are flooded with that love of which he alone is capable.…At that point the need to proclaim* [*this love*] *arises spontaneously, it becomes irrepressible.*[15]

CCC 429: *From this loving knowledge of Christ springs the desire to proclaim him, to "evangelise", and to lead others to the "yes" of faith in Jesus Christ.*

CCC 425: *The transmission of the Christian faith consists primarily in proclaiming Jesus Christ in order to lead others to faith in him. From the beginning, the first disciples burned with the desire to proclaim Christ: "We cannot but speak of what we have seen and heard." And they invite people of every era to enter the joy of their communion with Christ.*

---

[15] Pope Francis, Address, 30th November 2019.

Pope St John Paul II: *Only those who deeply know the Lord and are converted to his love can become courageous heralds and witnesses in every circumstance. Is it not precisely from knowing Christ, his person, his love and his truth that those who experience him personally feel an irresistible desire to proclaim him to everyone, to evangelise and to lead others in the discovery of the faith?*[16]

Personal reflection: transformation of life

One Friday when I was teaching Religious Education in a Catholic high school in Panama, three girls aged twelve approached me after class: "Mrs Mason, how do we meet Jesus?" They had been listening to me saying again and again that it was important to *know* the Lord Jesus, not just *know about* him. I asked them, "How do you get to know anyone?" and suggested that it was normally through speaking together and spending time with that person. I told them that God, too, wishes to communicate personally with us, and that he does that most clearly through the Bible which is his divine Word. So I recommended that when they each go home that weekend, they sit down with a Bible in a quiet place and speak to the Lord Jesus, asking him to please reply through his word, the Sacred Scriptures.

On the following Monday morning, the three girls ran excitedly into the classroom before the other students

[16] Pope John Paul II, Homily, 28th February 1999.

arrived: "Mrs Mason, we met the Lord!" I was amazed. "You did? How?" They told me they had followed my suggestion and each of them had sat down in their bedrooms with their Bibles and asked the Lord a question that was important to them; then, when they had opened their Bibles, their eyes had fallen upon a Scripture verse which was an answer to their particular inquiry. One of the girls had a marker on the relevant page and showed me what she had read. She had asked if her teacher was telling the truth about the Lord, and the verse she had immediately noticed was in Acts, concerning Apollos, telling how he "spoke accurately about Jesus".

The girls' excitement was due to their experience that the Lord was with them just as he promised ("I will be with you always") and was personally interested in them. They decided that from then on they would go to the school chapel every Wednesday at lunchtime, fasting instead of eating lunch, to pray that all the others in the school would meet Jesus, too.

Towards the end of that school year, some of the older students asked if they could have a retreat before their graduation. I spoke with a few people from our parish prayer group who themselves had encountered Jesus and were experienced in giving retreats, and we agreed on a weekend date at the convent in the hills above Panama City. Besides proclaiming the gospel, the adults gave their own testimonies. One couple with six children revealed that their marriage had broken down because of the husband's drinking and womanising. The wife had responded to her situation by surrendering herself in a deeper way to Jesus and joining the parish prayer group for support. Her husband had been so amazed by her peace and charity that eventually he had given his heart to the Lord, too, and the two of them had become mentors for others. After that testimony I overheard one of the girls say to another student, "Now I know why the Catholic Church doesn't permit divorce!"

On the Saturday evening we offered the students an opportunity to give their hearts to the Lord. As the adults waited prayerfully in the chapel, one by one each of the young people came in to pray in front of the Blessed Sacrament, and each one had a unique and powerful encounter with the Lord Jesus. Afterwards, the same girl who had made the comment about the Church's teaching on marriage ran to the telephone to call her parents: "It's all REAL!" she announced to them with joy and astonishment. One lad – the school basketball star – spent the entire night prostrate in front of the tabernacle. Another boy, who was kind and well-behaved but had never been baptised, told us that he saw his whole life pass before his eyes and was shown his need to repent and be born anew in the spirit. Interestingly, that boy was the son of wealthy and glamorous parents who were cocaine addicts. He had confided in me one day after class that he was extremely worried about their drug habit, and we had prayed together for them. Now the Lord was showing him through prayer that, like every human being, he also needed to repent in order to receive the salvation Jesus won for him by his death on the cross.

On the Monday morning after the retreat, these young people came to school filled with joy and hope. The basketball star and a girl who had been his arch-enemy walked arm-in-arm into the headteacher's office and asked if they could go into all the classrooms and tell the other students about Jesus and his love for them. The whole group told me that they wanted to continue praying at school, so I mentioned the Wednesday lunchtime prayer in the school chapel. That Wednesday, as the group filed into the chapel, the three 12-year-old girls looked up in amazement. "Girls," I said. "Here is the answer to your months of prayer and fasting."

Prayer of Surrender to Jesus

Lord Jesus, I confess that I am a sinner. I believe that you died for me and that you want to give me new life in you. Please forgive me and restore in me the graces and gifts you gave me at my baptism. I surrender my life to you and ask you to be my Lord. Come into my heart and help me respond to your love. Thank you, Lord Jesus. Amen.